DEREK PRINCE

the Pilgrim LEGACY

WHITAKER HOUSE

Publisher's note: This book was compiled from the extensive archive of Derek Prince's unpublished materials and was edited by the Derek Prince Ministries editorial team.

Unless otherwise indicated, all Scripture quotations are taken from the *New King James Version*, © 1979, 1980, 1982 by Thomas Nelson, Inc. Used by permission. All rights reserved. Scripture quotation marked (NIV) is taken from the *Holy Bible, New International Version*®, NIV®, © 1973, 1978, 1984, 2011 by Biblica, Inc.® Used by permission of Zondervan. All rights reserved worldwide. www.zondervan.com. The "NIV" and "New International Version" are trademarks registered in the United States Patent and Trademark Office by Biblica, Inc.® Scripture quotation marked (TLB) is taken from *The Living Bible*, © 1971. Used by permission of Tyndale House Publishers, Inc., Carol Stream, Illinois 60188. All rights reserved.

Personal pronouns and adjectives relating to God, Jesus, and the Holy Spirit in Scripture quotations from the *New International Version* and *The Living Bible* have been capitalized to correspond to the overall style used in this book. The forms LORD and GOD (in small caps) in Bible quotations represent the Hebrew name for God *Yahweh* (Jehovah), while *Lord* and *God* normally represent the name *Adonai*, in accordance with the Bible version used.

THE PILGRIM LEGACY

Derek Prince Ministries
P.O. Box 19501 • Charlotte, North Carolina 28219-9501
www.derekprince.org

ISBN: 978-1-64123-768-0 • eBook 978-1-64123-769-7
Printed in the United States of America
© 2021 by Derek Prince Ministries–International

Whitaker House
1030 Hunt Valley Circle • New Kensington, PA 15068
www.whitakerhouse.com

Library of Congress Control Number: 2021945817

No part of this book may be reproduced or transmitted in any form or by any means, electronic or mechanical—including photocopying, recording, or by any information storage and retrieval system—without permission in writing from the publisher. Please direct your inquiries to permissionseditor@whitakerhouse.com.

1 2 3 4 5 6 7 8 9 10 11 / 27 26 25 24 23 22 21

So they left that goodly and pleasant city which had been their resting place near twelve years; but they knew they were pilgrims, and looked not much on those things, but lift up their eyes to the heavens, their dearest country, and quieted their spirits.
—William Bradford, *Of Plymouth Plantation*

CONTENTS

Foreword 9
Introduction: A Story That Must Be Told 13
   1. Winds of Change 17
   2. The Power of a Seed 21
   3. The Principle of Sowing 25
   4. The Destiny of Nations 29
   5. How I Met the Pilgrims 37
   6. Key Pilgrim Leaders 41
   7. Pilgrim or Puritan? 47
   8. The Covenant Concept 51
   9. How the Pilgrims Prevailed 55
  10. The Pilgrims in Community 65

11. Returning to the Rock	75
12. Staying the Course	83
Notes	89
About the Author	93

FOREWORD

I was first introduced to Derek Prince as an author by my father, Arthur Jehle. After Dad's conversion to Christianity, he encouraged me to read Derek's *Foundation Series* when I came to faith in my freshman year of college in 1971. While at Barrington College in Barrington, Rhode Island (1971–1975), I listened to many cassette-tape teachings by Derek.

But it was not until 1976 that the name of Derek Prince in connection with the Pilgrims came to my attention. I discovered this linkage in the personal library of John G. Talcott, Jr., founder of the Plymouth Rock Foundation. There I first heard about the 1970 commemorative event in Plymouth, Massachusetts, when John Talcott, chair of the event, introduced Derek to the Pilgrims. Years later, I read Derek's own account of this experience in his book *Shaping History Through Prayer and Fasting*, and I remarked to myself, "Wow, I know that story."

Many years have passed since that first visit to John Talcott's library at The Pines in Plymouth. It inspired me to dig deeper into the history of the town in which I now live. I have spent over four decades studying many facets of the Pilgrims' saga. Their history, in its essence, is a church plant of believers who attempted to establish both a church and a commonwealth in the wilderness according to the Scriptures. This amazing group of individuals and families have had their applications of biblical faith examined and reexamined for centuries.

Much has been explored and articulated about the Pilgrims—from their system of government to their family life, economic activity, and relations with the Wampanoag. The archives of Pilgrim Hall Museum (the first public museum in America, begun in 1820 and still operating today in Plymouth) are filled with books brought by the Pilgrims on the *Mayflower*, written by them, or written about them.

What you are about to read in this short treatise by Derek Prince called *The Pilgrim Legacy* is an excellent articulation of the biblical principle of sowing and reaping as illustrated in their lives. Derek understood that, according to the Scriptures, the church of Jesus Christ is both a bride and a city. It has a vertical identity with Him but a horizontal responsibility, as salt and light, to influence the culture for good. In this book, Derek shows the reader the spiritual side of these believers, particularly their practice of prayer and fasting as a seed that would influence the growth of a nation. This is a unique articulation, but it is something that Derek picked up quite readily in the early 1970s as he read through William Bradford's *Of Plymouth Plantation*.

Consider that this small, remnant Pilgrim church did nothing of importance without first spending time in prayer, as well as calling days of humiliation (repentance) and fasting. They prayed about everything personally, and they prayed corporately before making key decisions, such as deciding who would leave for the New World and the business decision on financing the voyage. They also corporately prayed, with fasting, before departing from Delftshaven, Netherlands, for the New World. Upon their arrival at Cape Cod (Provincetown), "they fell upon their knees and blessed the God of Heaven."[1] Suffice it to say that the Pilgrims were, indeed, people of prayer. Their days of humiliation and fasting were significant, for they impacted not just their personal lives, but also the life of their community, as illustrated in this book.

If you find yourself in need of encouragement right now, please read *The Pilgrim Legacy*. Though we live in a time of sobriety due to the increase of spiritual darkness and a loss of liberty, this book will encourage you that the beginning answers we seek may seem small and insignificant, but they won't end there. It is thus important to realize that the real legacy of the Pilgrims is not just our nation, its unique religious and civil liberty, and its missionary call of sending people out to preach the gospel all over the world. It is a legacy of faith that begins in the heart, put there by a loving God through His Son, Jesus Christ. As articulated and so simply portrayed by Derek Prince, it begins in the heart as a small seed. Mark 4:31–32 says:

> [Faith] *is like a mustard seed which, when it is sown on the ground, is smaller than all the seeds on earth; but when it is sown, it grows up and becomes greater than all herbs, and shoots out large branches, so that the birds of the air may rest under its shade.*

The Pilgrims' story is one that illustrates how eternal ideas are like seeds that, when properly planted, bring forth great outcomes. As you read this book, remember that all great results begin small. But when initiated in faith toward the God of creation and our Redeemer, Jesus Christ, they can end up large enough to influence the destiny of nations. As William Bradford himself declared:

> Thus out of small beginnings greater things have been produced by His hand that made all things of nothing, and gives being to all things that are; and, as one small candle may light a thousand, so the light here kindled hath shone unto many, yea in some sort to our whole nation; let the glorious name of Jehovah have all the praise.[2]

—*Dr. Paul Jehle*
President, Plymouth Rock Foundation
Senior Pastor, The New Testament Church
Plymouth, MA

INTRODUCTION: A STORY THAT MUST BE TOLD

In his farewell address on January 11, 1989, U.S. President Ronald Reagan returned to one of his favorite themes for describing America. He spoke again of the nation as "a city set on a hill." These lofty words—taken directly from the Bible (see Matthew 5:15)—consistently struck a resonant chord in the hearts of all who heard them. On this occasion, Reagan expanded on this theme: "And she's still a beacon, still a magnet for all who must have freedom, for all the pilgrims from all the lost places who are hurtling through the darkness, toward home."[3]

A DEEPER REASON

How does a nation become one of the greatest and most powerful in the history of the free world? How does such a country become a light—a beacon for the lost pilgrims of the earth who are seeking a home? Some have argued that America's power and greatness are due to her abundant natural resources, combined with the heroic efforts and sacrifices of her people. This line of reasoning suggests that all its success is the result of fortuitous circumstances. But the reason is much deeper than mere coincidence. From the very beginning, the bright light that has shone from this nation has been powered from one source: an underlying faith in the living God. From its earliest days, America has been the "great experiment." It began as a representative republic, a land ruled not by a monarchy, aristocracy, or tyranny but by laws written down in her constitution. This declaration of principles remains a remarkable document, hewn by men of great wisdom who were guided by the truths of God's eternal Word.

A SHIFT IN PHILOSOPHY

The light of this nation—which President Reagan spoke of in his farewell address—is still shining. But something is going wrong. Like a heavy, unanticipated fog, there is a darkness gradually moving in to dim that light, that beacon known as "America." Instead of reflecting the light of Jesus Christ—the Light of the World—this country seems to be leading the world away from that light toward darkness: the dark philosophy of secular humanism.

What has happened? Why has America turned from its biblical foundations—from honoring God and His Word?

Why is this nation now seemingly bent on removing the recognition of God and the Bible from the public square? These are questions that must be addressed.

God has used America to bless the nations of the world, and countless people from those countries have made the journey to this land to become her citizens. One such man was Derek Prince, a well-known scholar and Bible teacher from England. At first, Derek knew nothing about the founding of America beyond a brief sketch he had learned from English schoolbooks. All of that changed, however, in the early 1970s.

In the pages that follow, Derek will share with us how, as a Britisher, he discovered the story of the Pilgrims. As he learned of their heroic struggle for religious freedom that led to the founding of this country, the unexpected truths he encountered made an impact on his own life. Derek became convinced that the legacy of the Pilgrims was a story that must be told.

This saga must not be erased from the history of America or from the public squares of nations throughout the world. What will keep the Pilgrim record from being extinguished by an encroaching agenda of darkness?

In many ways, that question is the basis for this book, dedicated to the Pilgrims and their unfading light. That light—the light of Christ—burned in the hearts of America's Pilgrims. And it is still shining today.

His life is the light that shines through the darkness—and the darkness can never extinguish it. (John 1:5 TLB)

—The International Publishing Team
of Derek Prince Ministries

ONE

WINDS OF CHANGE

I grew up in England in a military family where it was customary to send boys away to school at around the age of nine or ten—sometimes even younger. These days, that sounds almost cruel to some people. But, in those days, it was the custom. I took to academic life very well and enjoyed a good measure of success.

Like most traditional families in Britain, we were Anglican. While I was attending Eton College, the time came for me to be confirmed in the Anglican church. I was about the age of fifteen, and my father required that I go through the necessary classes to be confirmed with the other boys. Although I did what my father wanted, inwardly, I rebelled. I found religion utterly boring and illogical. By the time I reached Cambridge University, where I chose philosophy as my field of study, I had shed all vestiges of any kind of faith.

OUT OF HUMANISM

My strong academic background in philosophy immersed me in the humanistic spirit of the modern age. In fact, when I first encountered the principles presented in the Bible, I was essentially a confirmed agnostic. I had never read the Bible. I didn't even own one. With the onset of World War II, however, I had to suspend my promising academic future as a professor of philosophy at Cambridge University to enlist as a conscientious objector in the British Army.

As I packed my belongings, at the last minute, I obtained a big, black King James Version of the Bible to take with me. My reasons for making this choice were typically practical. Since I had never read it, I needed to know it to refute it. My review of the Bible would be a purely intellectual exercise. I even thought reading it might make me a better philosopher. Also, because of the length of this "book," it would take many months to finish it.

THE ENCOUNTER

Like every other book on philosophy I had ever read, I started at the beginning—in Genesis. As I ventured into the story of creation, reading how the Spirit of God was hovering over the waters, little did I realize that this same creative Spirit was also hovering over the chaos and emptiness in my own heart and soul. At the same time I was reading the Bible, I was completely unaware that it was also "reading" me—quietly penetrating the innermost part of my being. Finally, one unforgettable night when I was alone in my barracks, the One I had been reading about in the Bible—Jesus, the Messiah, the Son of God—revealed Himself to me. My life was changed forever. I was marvelously converted and eventually answered God's call upon me to enter full-time Christian ministry.

Since that amazing moment when I personally encountered Jesus Christ, I have based my entire life and ministry on the Word of God. My own testimony is that the Bible is entirely reliable, trustworthy, and true. All of my research, lessons, and teachings are drawn straight from the Scriptures. Seldom have I made reference to any other source, historical or otherwise.

A POWERFUL EXAMPLE

In a sense, this book maintains that same biblical focus. What I share here will be drawn primarily from Scripture. On this occasion, however, I will also focus extensively on the historical record of the Pilgrims—in particular, the famous work by William Bradford, *Of Plymouth Plantation*. The truths that are resident in the Pilgrim narratives are powerful examples of how foundational principles in the Christian faith can be applied in a real and practical way to our circumstances today—and to the world situation at this time in history.

During my days in the British Army, as I was working my way through the Bible, my imagination was stirred by what I read. I was captivated by the story of how God called forth a people from Abraham—how, from a small band of sojourners in a foreign land, He built a great nation. In much the same way, my imagination was captivated by the story of a small band of Europeans, the Pilgrims—who were also called by God, and who also sojourned in a foreign land to become a great nation.

In *The Pilgrim Legacy*, as you and I look back to the arrival of the Pilgrims in the New World, it is a good time for us to look to the rock from which all Americans were hewn. As we retrace those steps, it will also reveal where we have strayed from the path. Will we be able to humble ourselves and repent for detours we have taken that would have grieved our forefathers—mistakes that have definitely grieved our heavenly Father?

Therefore, as we read the story of the Pilgrims, let's pray and humbly ask that, once again, God will lead us. Let us ask Him to save us from the attack of enemies without and—even more importantly now—enemies within. This book is offered with deep gratitude for the example our Pilgrim ancestors left us. They fought the good fight—and won. May God grant us that same victory.

TWO

THE POWER OF A SEED

When we consider the historic greatness of America, it is hard to imagine the smallness of its origins. But that is the nature of most beginnings—they start with something small, like a seed.

What was the initial "seed" of our nation? Who planted it? Did they have any idea that from such a small seed would grow one of the greatest countries in the history of the world?

LIVING TRUTHS

At its core, the Pilgrim saga is the account of how they laid a foundation upon which the nation of America was built. As you read their story, you will see one simple, prevailing truth: the lasting legacy the Pilgrims left came from their faithful adherence to powerful, universal principles found in the Word of God—the Bible.

It is impossible to separate the truths of Scripture from the lives of this small band of sojourners. Indeed, these are truths that still live today. With that perspective in mind, we can discover how our Pilgrim brothers and sisters put these principles into practice as the foundation upon which the United States of America was built.

Why is this important? Because in all the history of the world, as nations have arisen and fallen amid endless wars and bloodshed, the founding of America was utterly unique. It had never happened before, and it has never happened since. Reaching the shores of an unknown wilderness, a small group of people planted seeds—not seeds of military might, wealth, or power but seeds of faith and freedom. And those seeds took root and grew.

Let's find out why.

THE LENS OF SCRIPTURE

As I mentioned in the previous chapter, during my years of academic life at Cambridge, I was a confirmed agnostic with absolutely no interest in the Bible. When I became a Christian, however, the Bible became the basis for all that I believed and taught. I am firmly convinced that the Word of God holds important, enduring truths that can be applied to our lives today. These principles have been influential throughout time and history—indeed, throughout the whole world.

In their own time in history, the Pilgrims viewed all of life through the lens of Scripture. For example, one of the biblical principles we will examine in this book is about seeds and sowing, a very familiar part of the everyday life of the English settlers. We see this principle illustrated in the New Testament book of Galatians, chapter 6, verses 7 and 8:

> *Do not be deceived, God is not mocked; for whatever a man sows, that he will also reap. For he who sows to his flesh will of the flesh reap corruption, but he who sows to the Spirit will of the Spirit reap everlasting life.*

"You reap what you sow." Haven't we all used that phrase at one time or another? One of the key principles of this book and the Pilgrim history is based on this phrase: "Whatever a man sows, that he will also reap."

In the passage quoted above, the apostle Paul, who wrote Galatians, was imparting profound truth in a practical way—a pattern seen throughout the Bible. Taking a principle from the natural realm—that of sowing seed—Paul was applying it to the unseen, supernatural realm: the unseen realm of the Spirit. Like all universal truths, this principle will apply in every area of life where we can, in any sense, talk of "seed."

FROM THE BEGINNING

The Pilgrims understood that, in the mind of God, this concept of "seed" is very important. How do we know this? Because it is actually one of the initial principles God instituted in creation. Everything reproduces after its kind, according to the seed that is found in it. Since the third day of creation, this principle has not changed. Here is what we read in the very first chapter of Genesis:

> Then God said, "Let the earth bring forth grass, the herb that yields seed, and the fruit tree that yields fruit according to its kind, whose seed is in itself, on the earth"; and it was so. And the earth brought forth grass, the herb that yields seed according to its kind, and the tree that yields fruit, whose seed is in itself according to its kind. And God saw that it was good. So the evening and the morning were the third day. (Genesis 1:11–13)

Hours could be spent on gleaning the truths of this passage! For our purposes here, however, I will just point out three interrelated parts of this principle. First, if you want to reproduce, you have to have seed. Second, if you want seed, you have to produce fruit, "whose seed is in itself." Third, wherever you find seed and reproduction, that process will always culminate in like reproducing like, "according to its kind."

In the face of current scientific theory, the biblical viewpoint that like reproduces like is not a popular way of thinking. Even so, the evidence of the world around us seems to support the biblical principle God laid out in Genesis: like begets like. If you plant an apple seed, you will never get an orange tree. But if you plant an orange seed, you will get an orange tree. For human beings, this principle goes far beyond agriculture, horticulture, and the animal kingdom. It also applies to the spiritual realm.

THREE

THE PRINCIPLE OF SOWING

In 2 Corinthians, the apostle Paul applies this universal truth of seeds producing according to their own kind to other practical areas of life. In that regard, let's look briefly at two verses in chapter 9:

> *But this I say: He who sows sparingly will also reap sparingly, and he who sows bountifully will also reap bountifully. So let each one give as he purposes in his heart, not grudgingly or of necessity; for God loves a cheerful giver.*
> (2 Corinthians 9:6–7)

THE WISE SOWER

In the agricultural society of Paul's day and time, the entire community depended on successful farming. Everyone knew that a wise farmer would never take good seed and walk down the main street of the town casting it into the gutter. Why not? Because, in the gutter, it would not reproduce. But if that same farmer would find the proper soil and sow the proper seed, under the right conditions, that seed would reproduce many times over. That is good, basic agricultural theory, isn't it?

Building on that principle, Paul redirects our focus in verse 7 from farming to another kind of sowing—giving to God's work: *"So let each one give as he purposes in his heart, not grudgingly or of necessity; for God loves a cheerful giver."* Paul is saying that what works for successful farming will work for philanthropic giving.

The same principle applies to business as well. If you find a good investment (whether it is a business, a charity, or a ministry), you make sure the conditions are right, you pray, and you invest—and eventually you will reap according to what you have sown. If you sow sparingly, you will reap sparingly. If you sow bountifully, you will reap bountifully. What you sow in good soil will always be multiplied. But here is the principle: *what you sow is what gets multiplied.* If you sow nickels, you will reap multiplied nickels. If you sow dollars, you will reap multiplied dollars. If you sow hundreds of dollars, you will reap multiplied hundreds of dollars.

This is an absolute fact. It is just as certain as the laws that govern raising crops or livestock. People who are sometimes reluctant to invest in a worthy cause or who are stingy in their giving do not realize this kind of multiplication. They have never understood that this is the way you sow. Then they wonder why there is no fruit! If you and I want to reap, we have to start by sowing.

TWO CONCLUSIONS

There are two conclusions we can draw from the verses cited above. First, the principle of sowing and reaping has universal application, reaching far beyond the natural realm. Second, *in every area of life*, if we want to reap, we have to start by sowing. But we will only reap if we begin with good seed.

At this point, you may be wondering, "Why all this emphasis on sowing and reaping? What does this have to do with a nation's history?" Simply put, we don't want to overlook the powerful truths that lie hidden behind the basic act of sowing a seed. (Sometimes, the most powerful truths are easy to miss because they seem so simple.)

Throughout the Bible, God often hides His eternal truths and wisdom in this way for us to discover. Jesus pointed this out when He prayed, *"I praise You, Father, Lord of heaven and earth, because You have hidden these things from the wise and learned, and revealed them to little children. Yes, Father, for this is what You were pleased to do"* (Matthew 11:25–26 NIV).

Let's make sure that, in our own personal lives and decisions, we give proper place to this powerful principle. It's important not to underestimate its significance. Instead, let's continue to discover what our Pilgrim forefathers knew: if we want to reap, we have to sow. But we must start with good seed.

FOUR

THE DESTINY OF NATIONS

In our discussion thus far, perhaps some memories of certain events in your own life have come to mind. It may be that certain decisions you have made (which would be a kind of sowing) did not have the outcome you had hoped for (which would be a kind of reaping). When we look at our own individual histories under the light of this principle, it can reveal some profound personal truths to us.

A WIDER APPLICATION

I believe, however, that this examination can take us far beyond the life of the individual. There is a process of sowing and reaping in history that reflects the biblical truth we have just considered. The more closely we look at the histories of nations, the more we see this principle at work.

> *For as the earth brings forth its bud, as the garden causes the things that are sown in it to spring forth, so the Lord God will cause righteousness and praise to spring forth before all the nations.*

This hopeful passage speaks about sowing and reaping in the earth and in the nations. It is not restricted to individuals. What God has caused to be sown in history will be reaped in history. Where seeds have been sown in history that bring forth righteousness and praise, the harvest will be manifested in history. As the passage states, *"The Lord God will cause righteousness and praise to spring forth before all the nations."* Truly, this principle extends far beyond the lives of individuals. It is a promise to the nations.

A PREVAILING PLAN

God's heart for the nations is further revealed in another passage from the Bible, Psalm 33:10–11:

> *The Lord brings the counsel of the nations to nothing; He makes the plans of the peoples of no effect. The counsel of the Lord stands forever, the plans of His heart to all generations.*

No matter what plans nations and their respective governments formulate, their intentions will never come to lasting fulfillment if those plans stand in opposition to the counsel of the Lord. In the final analysis, it is God's plan and God's purpose that will prevail. This truth applies not merely to individuals but to nations as well. Verse 12 of this passage makes that application clear:

> *Blessed is the nation whose God is the* LORD, *the people He has chosen as His own inheritance.* (Psalm 33:12)

SHAPING A DESTINY

As we can plainly see, in the same way that God has a purpose and a plan for individuals, He has one for the nations. Can you believe this is the case? Do you believe nations have a destiny? The Bible clearly teaches that this principle is true.

Perhaps you would agree that, as individuals, we each have a destiny. No two of us are alike in our destinies, but each of us has a part in shaping our own destiny. I am convinced the same is true of nations. Nations have destinies. As with humans, these destinies are not all alike. But, as with humans, each nation plays a part in shaping its own destiny.

How does a nation participate in shaping its own destiny? In the same way an individual does. Essentially, it is through the process of sowing and reaping. What nations sow, they will reap. If they seek to align themselves with the purposes of God, they will experience the favor and blessing of God. But if they seek to align themselves with purposes that are in opposition to those of God, they will be broken. They will not prosper.

A good example from recent history that illustrates this truth would be the events that unfolded surrounding the nations of Great Britain and Israel after World War II. Here is the principle we see at work: any nation that directs its strength and resources in opposition to God's purposes for Israel will ultimately be broken. I haven't the faintest doubt in my mind that this is true—and I will tell you why.

AN EMPIRE DIMINISHES

As a Britisher, I saw this very phenomenon occur in my lifetime. I was born in 1915 in Bangalore, India, at a time when India was a British protectorate and the brightest jewel in the British crown. In this period of history, the British Empire was at its zenith, having dominated the world for nearly one hundred years. During this influential period, one could look at any map of the globe and see the domination and presence of Great Britain in either hemisphere, indicated by the color pink. Every area shaded pink signified that Britain claimed dominion over it—and there were many such areas.

Amazingly, by 1947, the British Empire had largely dissipated. After playing a pivotal role in leading the allied forces to victory in World War II, the whole British Empire fell apart within ten years. Undeniably, World War II had taken a heavy toll on Great Britain. But, in my opinion, there was a much more significant reason behind the disintegration of this great entity.

Do you know the moment when it really began to fall apart? I believe it was when Great Britain withstood God's purposes for Israel in Palestine. According to my understanding of scriptural truth, this was the undeniable cause and effect behind the fall of the British Empire. It is very important for people of every nation to bear this in mind. In Isaiah 60:12, God says this to the Jewish people in Zion: *"For the nation and kingdom which will not serve you shall perish, and those nations shall be utterly ruined."*

Whatever a nation plans, it must not get on the wrong side of Israel. Without a doubt, Israel will survive. But any nation that stands against it might not.

We can be thankful that, in large part, the United States of America has continued to stand with Israel. To this day, I believe we still enjoy the blessing and protection of God because we have historically aligned ourselves with God's will, as revealed in Scripture, concerning Israel.

It is important for us to remember, however, that we cannot take credit for assuming this biblical position. This perspective did not begin with us. It originated primarily from the seeds of God's Word, planted hundreds of years ago by our Pilgrim forefathers into the soil of our nation. In many ways, we have reaped blessings where we did not sow.

REAPING WHERE WE HAVE NOT SOWN

Jesus Himself spoke to His disciples about this principle of reaping where one has not sown. In a scene described in the fourth chapter of John, the disciples arrived at the Samaritan village where Jesus had just met with the woman at the well. They soon witnessed a tremendous public response to Jesus's presence and message.

In some ways, this response should not be considered unusual. Jesus was always drawing crowds of people. So why was this situation in Samaria different? It was different because centuries of animosity had existed between the Samaritans and the Jews. Both groups went to great lengths to avoid each other. Yet, based on the single testimony of the woman at the well, the whole village in Samaria came out to see Jesus, the Man who had told her *"all things that I ever did"* (John 4:29). Many of the villagers said that after being with Jesus, they believed in Him as the Messiah. (See verse 42.) It was in this context that Jesus pointed out the following lesson to His disciples:

> *For in this the saying is true: "One sows and another reaps." I sent you to reap that for which you have not labored; others have labored, and you have entered into their labors.* (John 4:37–38)

The disciples had seen a dramatic response to the message of the Messiah. All well and good. But Jesus was intent that they understand something more. Essentially, what Jesus said was, "Don't imagine that this response is due solely to your presence or your ministry. There has been a long process of preparation leading to this moment. Other men and women labored. Other men and women sowed the seed over the centuries. What they sowed in those past years, you are reaping now."

SOWING THROUGH THE CENTURIES

Although there is no actual comment to this effect in the gospel of John, my personal opinion is that the other people to whom Jesus was referring were the Old Testament sages, prophets, and teachers who, over long centuries and in the purposes of God, sowed seed into Israel. Now, when the Messiah had come, the harvest time was taking place. The early church would reap the result of seed that had been sown by men and women who had served long before their time.

We see the same principle unfolding in the lives and destinies of nations. It is the phenomenon in the process of sowing and reaping where one reaps where he or she has not sown. It may take many generations, but eventually the harvest comes forth.

Every American needs to understand this principle in regard to their spiritual inheritance. Seed that was sown by our Pilgrim ancestors over four hundred years ago is still producing a harvest—even now.

Exactly what was that seed? What were the truths and principles the Pilgrims so earnestly sowed into the spiritual soil of this nation? To answer that question, we need to go back in history. We need to retrace the earliest days of America. We need to get a firsthand look at the life and times of the Pilgrim settlers. In the next chapter, we will begin that journey.

FIVE

HOW I MET THE PILGRIMS

As I mentioned earlier in this book, I am British by birth. When I first came to the United States, I knew almost nothing about the Pilgrims. Their experience and influence were a complete blank in the historical education I had received in Britain. It wasn't long, however, before I came to understand that the personal and family celebrations in America during the week of the Thanksgiving holiday centered on the Pilgrim fathers and mothers. These brave souls first landed on the coast of America in 1620, and they were, in a certain sense, the spiritual ancestors of this nation.

AN AMAZING DISCOVERY

Some years after I had come to the United States, I became an American citizen. Not long after that experience, I was invited to be the speaker at a commemorative event at

Plymouth Plantation in Massachusetts. Much to my surprise, this trip to Plymouth became a decisive moment in my life. Through that event, I came into direct contact with the story of the Pilgrims, and I was deeply moved by their lives and history. Their story became a part of mine, inspiring what I believe to be one of the most important books I have ever written: *Shaping History Through Prayer and Fasting*.

The following excerpt from that book is the account—in my own words—of how and why all of this came about. Why am I including this information? It is my conviction that the truths I am about to share have a very important application to our nations today. Here is how it all began.

> In 1970 and 1971, the city of Plymouth, Massachusetts, celebrated the 350th anniversary of the landing of the Pilgrims at that point on the coast of America. A special committee was appointed by the city to organize various kinds of celebrations that were appropriate to the occasion. This committee paid me the honor of inviting me to give a series of addresses in the Church of the Pilgrimage in the city of Plymouth.
>
> During my visit [to Plymouth], two members of the committee were kind enough to show me the main places of historical interest and also to introduce me to some of the original records of the period of the Pilgrims. In this way, I became acquainted for the first

time with the history *Of Plymouth Plantation* written by William Bradford.

Background of the Pilgrims

Having been educated in Britain, I do not recall ever having learned anything at school about the Pilgrims. The term "Pilgrim Fathers," commonly used by Americans, had created in my mind a vague impression of severe old men with long white beards, probably attired in dark formal clothing similar to that associated with ministers of religion. I was surprised to discover that the majority of the Pilgrims at the time of their arrival in America were still young men and women. For example, William Bradford was thirty one years old in 1621, when he was first appointed governor of the colony. Most of the other Pilgrims were about the same age or younger.…

As I studied Bradford's firsthand account of the founding of Plymouth Colony and its early struggles, I developed a strong sense of spiritual kinship with him and his fellow Pilgrims. I discovered that their whole way of life was based upon the systematic study and application of the Scriptures. With the main conclusions and convictions to which this study led them, I found myself in complete accord. In fact, they are in close agreement with some of the main themes developed in this book.[4]

I found William Bradford's book, *Of Plymouth Plantation*, to be a fascinating eyewitness account of the origins of the Pilgrims in England. It proved to be a gripping narrative of their arduous journey to North America, along with all the hardships and struggles they experienced once they arrived.

After my visit to Plymouth, however, I was surprised that so few people had even heard of this book, much less actually read it. So, throughout this treatise, I will unapologetically quote from Bradford's book. Why? Because it so closely relates to the theme of our study in this book. The passages I especially want to share with you—many of which I included in my book *Shaping History Through Prayer and Fasting*—are included throughout the remainder of this volume.

SIX

KEY PILGRIM LEADERS

We will begin this section by tracing the life of the man who became the second governor[5] of Plymouth Colony and who wrote the book *Of Plymouth Plantation*. I suppose that, in many ways, William Bradford eventually became the overall leader of the entire expedition.

One of the first aspects of his life that I noticed was his love for the Bible. As we saw from the excerpt in our previous chapter, the seed of the Word of God was deeply sown in this man's life. That seed in William Bradford may very well be where the Christian roots of the nation of America began.

WILLIAM BRADFORD

Having grown up myself in England, I knew that Bradford is a very good English name. In fact, it is the name of a well-known city in the historical county of Yorkshire, the same county where Bradford was born.

William Bradford was spiritually mature for his age—remarkably so. Although he had been born into an influential farming family, he was orphaned by the time he was seven years old and was sent to live with his uncles. A somewhat sickly boy, he spent many hours reading classic literature. By the age of twelve, he was also known for being an avid reader of the Bible, which could account for his being also drawn to Puritan theology. (We will discuss the differences between the Pilgrims and the Puritans in the next chapter.)

By the age of sixteen, Bradford had become an active member of a Separatist home church. This was remarkable in itself, since it was not a congregation his family approved of. The whole course of Bradford's life was determined by the spiritual depth and experiences of his boyhood and early manhood. The following quote is from the introduction to *Of Plymouth Plantation* in the highly regarded Samuel E. Morrison edition of the work:

> William Bradford…was born at Austerfield, Yorkshire, in the early spring of 1590.… At the age of twelve he became a constant reader of the Bible—the Geneva version that he generally quotes—and when still a lad he was so moved by the Word as to join a group of Puritans who met for prayer and discussion at the house of William Brewster in the nearby village of Scrooby.[6]

For me personally, stemming from my leadership role in Christianity, especially in the 1960s and 1970s, I immediately recognized two similarities between William Bradford and many sincere Christian men and women I knew during those years: a deep commitment to Scripture and active participation in home prayer group meetings. Both of these aspects of Bradford's personal history are in line with the pivotal times of Christian renewal—especially during those decades to which I referred earlier.

> When this group, inspired by the Rev. Richard Clyfton, organized itself as a separate Congregational church in 1606 [when Bradford was sixteen years old], Bradford joined it despite "the wrath of his uncles" and the "scoff of his neighbors."[7]

These experiences from Bradford's early life reflect another similarity to what many Christians have experienced during times of renewal: the painful opposition from friends and family who don't understand their devotion and enthusiasm. Such opposition is especially targeted against those who attend home prayer meetings and join "strange" groups. For Bradford, it was this split-off group (known as "Separatists"), which he joined as a teenager, that was later to become known as the Pilgrims.

> From that date until his death half a century later, Bradford's life revolved around that of this church or congregation, first in Scrooby, next in the Low Countries and finally in New England.[8]

CAMBRIDGE BACKGROUNDS

Along with William Bradford, we will briefly examine the lives of three other ministers who shaped the theology and the purposes of the Pilgrims and Puritans. As I mentioned earlier in this book, before I came to faith in Jesus Christ, my own educational background was at Cambridge University. It was there that I earned my MA in philosophy and was elected to a fellowship at King's College around the time World War II broke out.

As grateful as I have been for my time at Cambridge, I had always wondered if anything of a distinctly Christian nature had ever come from that institution. For me, it was a thrilling discovery to learn that three godly men—all of whom were educated at Cambridge—went on to shape the faith of the Pilgrims and the future of America.

RICHARD CLYFTON

The first I would like to mention is Richard Clyfton, who formed the original congregation of Separatists from a home prayer group. This congregation would eventually become known as the Pilgrim Church.

Clyfton's inspired preaching reflected a deep desire for true religious liberty, and it attracted John Robinson, William Brewster, and the young William Bradford to his congregation. As time went on, strong relationships were forged among these men. All of them had a mutual desire for the religious freedom to study the Word of God and live according to its principles.

JOHN ROBINSON

The second of these three important leaders was John Robinson. He was ordained at Cambridge and, in 1607, became the assistant pastor of Clyfton's home church. By 1608, the escalating persecution in England forced the Separatists to escape and migrate to the city of Leyden (Leiden) in the Netherlands. John Robinson pastored the church through those very important but difficult years.

Although Robinson dreamed of going to the New World, when the first group set sail for America, he stayed behind in the Netherlands to serve those who could not go. He continued his profound influence upon the entire Pilgrim community through his prayers and letter writing. But he never made it to New England.

WILLIAM BREWSTER

The third leader, William Brewster, served as an elder for the congregation in Leyden. In that capacity, he made the journey on the Mayflower with the first wave of settlers from Leyden with William Bradford. In Plymouth, Massachusetts, he became the senior elder and (spiritual) leader of the community.

We can be extremely grateful for the marvelous way the Lord joined together the lives of William Bradford and these three men: Richard Clyfton, John Robinson, and William Brewster. As unexpected paths were unfolding before them, these men faithfully led this small group of Christians through perilous times.

Their lives are remarkable examples of true servant leadership. They could not have foreseen the impact their humble obedience and unfailing courage would ultimately have upon the history of the world.

SEVEN

PILGRIM OR PURITAN?

There is a great deal of general confusion regarding the differences between the Puritans and the Pilgrims. Some people mistakenly believe the terms are interchangeable—simply two different names for the same group of people. This misconception is understandable because Pilgrims and Puritans had many similarities.

Both religious groups faced severe persecution in England. Both groups sought religious freedom in the American colonies. In fact, they actually arrived in the colonies within ten years of each other. However, the viewpoint of the Pilgrims was significantly different from that of the Puritans.

REFORMATION AND RESTORATION

One of the most important ways the Pilgrims differed from the Puritans is outlined in the following paragraphs. The major difference I would point to is that the Puritans were determined to stay inside the institutional church. Their objective was *to reform it*—by force, if necessary.

The Pilgrims, on the other hand, had many of the same ideas as the Puritans. But they declined to force their beliefs on others. Above all, the Pilgrims wanted religious freedom. They desired to be separated from any form of governmental or legal compulsion in matters of religion. This guiding principle became a truly significant part of the foundation the Pilgrims laid for this country.

To better explain these important differences, let's look at a few more excerpts from my book *Shaping History Through Prayer and Fasting*:

> Although the Pilgrims were initially associated with the Puritans, there were important differences between them. Both saw the need of religious reform, but they differed concerning the means by which reform was to be achieved. The Puritans determined to remain within the established church and to impose reform from within—by compulsion, if necessary. The Pilgrims sought liberty for themselves, but declined to use the machinery of secular government to enforce their views upon others. These differing points of view are expressed in the following passage from Leonard Bacon's *Genesis of the New England Churches*.[9]

Bacon's excerpt, a rather beautiful passage, is quoted here:

In the Old World on the other side of the ocean, the Puritan was a Nationalist, believing that a Christian nation is a Christian church, and demanding that the Church of England should be thoroughly reformed; while the Pilgrim was a Separatist, not only from the Anglican Prayer-book and Queen Elizabeth's episcopacy, but from all national churches.... The Pilgrim wanted liberty for himself and his wife and little ones, and for his brethren, to walk with God in a Christian life as the rules and motives of such a life were revealed to him from God's Word. For that he went into exile; for that he crossed the ocean; for that he made his home in a wilderness. The Puritan's idea was not liberty, but right government in church and state—such government as should not only permit him, but also compel other men to walk in the right way.[10]

Here is the summary I offered for this point made by Bacon:

The difference between Puritans and Pilgrims could be expressed in the two words *reformation* and *restoration*. The Puritans sought to reform the church as it existed in their day. The Pilgrims believed that the ultimate purpose of God was to restore the church to its original condition, as portrayed in the New Testament. This shines forth clearly in the first paragraph of the first chapter of Bradford's book, where he expressed the Pilgrims' vision of restoration in the following words:[11]

> The churches of God revert to their ancient purity and recover their primitive [i.e., original] order, liberty and beauty.[12]

FOUR BEAUTIFUL WORDS

In Bradford's own words, we are given a picture of the four qualities the Pilgrims sought after: purity, order, liberty, and beauty. This was their vision of the church that Jesus will someday return to claim: not an old crone walking around with a cane but a beautiful bride who radiates *purity, order, liberty,* and *beauty.* That vision of the Pilgrims, expressed in those four words, is very appealing to me personally. It is exactly my hope for the church. Would you say the same?

Later in the opening chapter of his book, Bradford more fully explains the purpose and vision of the Pilgrims:

> [They labored] to have the right worship of God and discipline of Christ established in the church, according to the simplicity of the gospel, without the mixture of men's inventions; and to have and to be ruled by the laws of God's Word, dispensed in those offices, and by those officers of Pastors, Teachers and Elders, etc. according to the Scriptures.[13]

In my many years of ministry, this is the heart cry I have heard so many Christians express: *a genuine longing for this kind of New Testament authenticity, purity, and simplicity.*

EIGHT

THE COVENANT CONCEPT

One of the most vital truths we see operating in the lives of the Pilgrims is the principle of "covenant." The basis of the entire Pilgrim society was that they formed a covenant with one another and with God. On the basis of those covenants, they entered into what we would call a *community*.

Those two words—*covenant* and *community*—are key principles for us as Christians today. We are to be a community based on a covenant. In fact, any true community must be based upon the concept of a covenant. Every person must know what their responsibility is and how to function in it. One of the truths God is bringing back to us today is the importance of covenant.

LIVING SACRIFICIALLY

It is very significant that this concept was present in the Pilgrim mindset. Why? Because God operates on the basis of covenant. Every time He has done anything serious and permanent in human history, He has always done it with a covenant.

In Psalm 50:5, God says, *"Gather My saints together to Me, those who have made a covenant with Me by sacrifice."* That is the definition of God's faithful people: *those who have made a covenant with Him on the basis of a sacrifice.*

This is exactly what the Pilgrims did—they lived sacrificially for God and one another. From the beginning, the Pilgrims chose to join themselves into a close-knit community on the basis of covenant. Here are the words Bradford used to describe this formulation of the Pilgrim colony:

> [They] joined themselves (by a covenant of the Lord) into a church estate [what we would call a community], in the fellowship of the gospel, to walk in all His ways made known, or to be made known unto them, according to their best endeavours, whatsoever it should cost them, the Lord assisting them.[14]

A JOURNEY TOGETHER

The Pilgrims committed themselves completely to do whatever God would reveal to them from His Word—no matter what it might cost. It is significant to note that, in doing so, they did not claim to know it all. To me, this is one of the most refreshing characteristics about the Pilgrims—they never claimed to have "arrived." This distinguishes them from a large percentage of religious groups. (We will discuss this point in a later chapter.)

Bradford returned to the theme of the configuration of the Plymouth congregation. Here is how he spoke about the life of the Pilgrims in Leyden, Holland, after they escaped persecution in England:

> They came as near the primitive [original] pattern of the first churches as any other church[es] of these later times have done.[15]

Please pay special attention to these words in Bradford's description: *the primitive* [original] *pattern of the first churches.* This attribute was the Pilgrims' supreme objective. This is what they were after.

A COMMON PURPOSE

Bradford added to this sense of purpose later in his book when he commented on another reason for the Pilgrims' coming to America. Given that these words were written four hundred years ago, I find them extremely significant for our day. Here is what Bradford said was the Pilgrims' main motive for setting out on their history-making journey to a new land:

> Lastly (and which was not least), a great hope and inward zeal they had of laying some good foundation…

for the propagating and advancing the gospel of the kingdom of Christ in those remote parts of the world; yea, though they should be but even as stepping-stones unto others for the performing of so great a work.[16]

Here we see the Pilgrims' overarching objective: to open up the North American continent for the spreading of "the gospel of the kingdom of Christ." I like the fact that Bradford didn't just say "the gospel." He said "the gospel of the kingdom of Christ." It is significant that Jesus Christ Himself used this terminology in Matthew 24:14: *"And this gospel of the kingdom will be preached in all the world as a witness to all the nations."* There is a certain difference between preaching the gospel, and preaching the gospel of the kingdom. The *gospel of the kingdom* is a gospel of power, authority, and supernatural attestations.

Without question, this "great hope" of William Bradford and the Pilgrims has been fulfilled to a significant degree. America has definitely been a stepping-stone in spreading the light of the gospel of the kingdom of God around the world. But as the world grows darker, here is the question: Will that light continue to shine—in America and across the globe?

As we continue our study, perhaps there is more we can learn from our Pilgrim ancestors about enabling the light of the gospel of the kingdom of God to shine brighter and brighter. If the Pilgrims were with us today, what would they tell us to do?

NINE

HOW THE PILGRIMS PREVAILED

At this time in history, we find ourselves facing many challenges in a rapidly changing world. We don't really know what lies ahead—but we *do* know that we need wisdom to face it.

In the 1600s, the Pilgrims also found themselves in a changing world. At the time of their departure from England, Europe was in religious and political turmoil. As various factions vied for control, increasing persecution and difficulties had forced the Pilgrims to flee to Holland, or what was then known as the Republic of the United Netherlands. Now they were facing a treacherous journey across the ocean—to a strange land far from home. How did they prepare for the intense challenges ahead?

I believe that if the Pilgrims were still among us, and we had the opportunity to ask them that question, they would probably say that their most effective spiritual tool was *collective prayer and fasting*, which they did quite frequently (to *fast* means to abstain from food deliberately for spiritual purposes).

When I say *collective*, I mean they did not fast as individuals. The whole community proclaimed the day on which they would all fast and seek God. Apparently this practice included everyone—even the children.

FERVENCY AND TEARS

When the Pilgrims spoke about fasting, they used one particular word: *humiliation*. We see an example of this type of "humiliation" in the following verse from the Bible:

> *If My people who are called by My name will humble themselves, and pray and seek My face, and turn from their wicked ways, then I will hear from heaven, and will forgive their sin and heal their land.* (2 Chronicles 7:14)

The Pilgrims knew that to humble oneself, in biblical language, meant *to fast*. In fact, when they finally decided to leave Holland and begin their journey to the New World, the last order they gave before leaving was to proclaim a universal fast. Here is William Bradford's account of this moment from *Of Plymouth Plantation*:

> So being ready to depart, they had a day of solemn humiliation, their pastor [John Robinson] taking his text from Ezra viii.21: "And there at the river, by

Ahava, I proclaimed a fast, that we might humble ourselves before our God, and seek of him a right way for us, and for our children, and for all our substance." Upon which he [Robinson] spent a good part of the day very profitably and suitable to their present occasion [in other words, he taught them from the Bible]; the rest of the time was spent in pouring out prayers to the Lord with great fervency, mixed with abundance of tears.[17]

Even though the language used in this quote is rather antiquated English, it is vivid. In fact, I would say that Bradford's account is a fairly similar description of the 1960s and 1970s home prayer meetings I described earlier. Those meetings were marked by *"great fervency, mixed with an abundance of tears."*

The prayer times Bradford described here were not the ordinary "churchy" affair. They weren't casual occasions where three or four people would utter a prayer, and the rest would simply say "Amen"—with everyone heading for home shortly thereafter.

Here is what I wrote next in my book *Shaping History Through Prayer and Fasting*:

Bradford's use of the word *humiliation* indicates that the Pilgrims understood the scriptural connection… between fasting and self-humbling. Robinson's choice of the text from Ezra is singularly appropriate. Both in motivation and in experience, there is a close parallel between the Pilgrims embarking on their journey to the New World and Ezra's company of exiles returning from Babylon to Jerusalem to help in the restoration of the temple.[18]

MORE TRUTH AND LIGHT

The address John Robinson gave to the Pilgrims before they started their journey was recorded by Edward Winslow, one of the Pilgrims who was a passenger on the *Mayflower*.

The following is Winslow's paraphrased version of Robinson's address, which has been preserved in Verna M. Hall's *Christian History of the Constitution*. I have added a few notes to help make the archaic English a little clearer. Here is Edward Winslow's summary of what John Robinson said on this day of prayer and fasting in Leyden before the Pilgrims departed:

> We are now ere long to part asunder, and the Lord knoweth whether he [Robinson] should live to see our face again. [Actually, Robinson never made it to America.] But whether the Lord had appointed it or not, he charged us before God and His blessed angels, to follow him no further than he followed Christ; and if God should reveal anything to us by any other instrument of His, to be as ready to receive it, as ever we were to receive any truth by his ministry [In other words, Robinson said, "I don't have it all. If anybody

comes with the truth of God's Word, receive it from them."]; for he was very confident the Lord had more truth and light yet to break forth out of His holy Word. He took occasion also miserably to bewail the state and condition of the Reformed churches [that is, the churches that were brought into being by the Reformation] who were come to a period [standstill] in religion, and would go no further than the instruments of their reformation [i.e., those who had been leaders in the Reformation].

As for example, the Lutherans, they could not be drawn to go beyond what Luther saw; for whatever part of God's will He had further imparted and revealed to Calvin, they [the Lutherans] will rather die than embrace it. And so also, saith he, you see the Calvinists [we would say Presbyterians], they stick where he [Calvin] left them, a misery much to be lamented; for though they were precious shining lights in their times, yet God had not revealed His whole will to them; and were they now living, saith he, they would be as ready and willing to embrace further light, as that they had received.[19]

WILLING TO GO FURTHER

Isn't there great truth in what John Robinson stated? Religious groups today tend to hide behind a previous generation who were reformers, innovators, and pioneers. Those groups say, "We will not go any further than they did." But the Pilgrims were willing to go further than the people before them. Christians of various denominations today do the greatest possible disservice to Luther, Calvin, and Wesley by hiding behind them and making them an excuse for not obeying truth revealed from the Word of God. Had these reformers been in our place, they would have obeyed it.

Here is the last paragraph of Winslow's description of the words of John Robinson:

> Here also he put us in mind of our church covenant, at least that part of it whereby we promise and covenant with God and one another [that is very significant: we covenant not only with God, but with one another] to receive whatsoever light or truth shall be made known to us from His written Word; but withal [he] exhorted us to take heed what we received for truth, and well to examine and compare it and weigh it with other Scriptures of truth before we received it.[20]

Do you see how balanced that is? Robinson says, "We don't know it all. There is more truth to come." We must be willing to receive truth. However, before receiving it, we must always compare it with Scripture to make sure it is biblically sound. Here is Winslow's last statement:

> For saith he [Robinson], it is not possible [that] the Christian world should come so lately [recently] out

of such thick antichristian darkness, and that full perfection of knowledge should break forth at once.[21]

What Robinson was clearly saying to these departing Pilgrims is that there is more to know. I will sum up with my own comment on this point from *Shaping History*:

> John Robinson's message on this occasion sums up the essence of the Pilgrims' theological position. This is indicated by their very choice of the name *Pilgrims*. They did not claim to have arrived at a final understanding of all truth. They were on a pilgrimage, looking for the further revelation of truth that lay ahead as they walked in obedience to truth already received.[22]

Most religious groups, having discovered truth, go on to say, "And that's all there is." That is their big mistake—one which, with John Robinson's help, the Pilgrims were able to avoid.

RAISING UP THE CHURCH

To my way of thinking, the church of Jesus Christ is like a great building that is being raised up, story by story, to completion. Every time God wants another story built, He finds a group of people who are committed, fearless, and faithful. To those people, God assigns the task of building another story. This idea applies completely to the Pilgrims. They were committed, fearless, and faithful people who were willing to build for God.

The Pilgrims, as Robinson's words indicate, recognized that there are two building assignments that are reserved for Jesus Christ alone: laying the foundation and putting on the roof. This is confirmed by the words spoken about Zerubbabel in Zechariah 4:9, where it says, *"The hands of Zerubbabel have laid the foundation…; his hands shall also finish it."*

I would say that the big mistake a majority of religious movements in the church make is this: having added their story to the building that God has called them to add, they take an additional, unauthorized step. What do they do next?

They put on the roof.

God never authorized them to do that. In putting on the roof, these groups are saying, "That's all there is. Here is our statement of fundamentals. This is what you're allowed to believe, and no more." By believing in this way, they go beyond divine authority.

BLOWING OFF THE ROOF

Please let me tell you briefly what will happen. The next time the wind of the Holy Spirit moves in the church, what is the first thing He will do? He will blow off the roof. Then God will raise up another group, and He will say to them, "Now it's time for you to lay the next story."

Who will be the primary opponents of the new group? *The group that built the last story.* Why? Because they are so anxious about their roof. All they want to do is hold on to the status quo, saying, "Don't take off our roof. We laid it, and it needs to stay in place." Unfortunately, this process is still taking place in the church today.

The Pilgrims could have clung to that kind of attitude. As they followed the Lord in renewal out of their religious convictions, they could have built a roof and settled forever in the Netherlands. Or, they could even have gone back to England and eventually built a roof there. But they had made a covenant with God and with one another. They agreed together to move forward in God's will, no matter the cost, and with God assisting them.

We can all be thankful that this *is* what they did—in the belief that their work would be the foundation for new truth and light that would come after them.

TEN

THE PILGRIMS IN COMMUNITY

So far in this book, we have learned a great deal about what the Pilgrims believed. Their practice of self-government and tolerance of differing points of view in their day, which was different from the Puritans, laid a strong foundation for religious freedom in the nation of America that was unparalleled in the history of the world. The Pilgrims had a deep belief in prayer and fasting, which sustained them as they faced the challenges of persecution in England, the treacherous journey across an ocean, and the unknown dangers in the New World. There is so much more to their story: how they arrived safely, how God protected them, and how they depended upon Him time and time again in periods of desperation when they had no recourse but to pray.

Time will not allow us to cover all the remarkable aspects of their history in this book. Thankfully, we have the complete historical record as a reference tool. I would, however, like to look at some specific challenges the Pilgrims faced as they labored to build the foundation of a nation.

A COMMUNAL EXPERIMENT

When they first arrived in the New World, the Pilgrims settled on a plan that we would call *communal living*. Due to the change in their financial contract, which was forced upon them prior to their sailing from England, there was little private ownership of land. Though they had desired a different arrangement, property ownership was allotted to the community, and, as a community, everyone had to work the land—regardless of who reaped the benefits of their efforts. As a result of this arrangement, during each winter of their first three years, the Pilgrims nearly starved to death. Here is what William Bradford wrote as they faced starvation in 1623:

> So they began to think how they might raise as much corn as they could, and obtain a better crop than they had done, that they might not still thus languish in misery. At length, after much debate of things [what we might call a "church fight"], the Governor (with the advice of the chiefest amongst them) gave way that they should set [plant] corn every man for his own particular [every man planting his own crop], and in that regard trust to themselves; in all other things to go on in the general way as before.[23]

What the Pilgrims were facing in this situation was the age-old conflict between individualism and communal living. How did they resolve this conflict? Bradford tells us in the following excerpts.

> And so [the Governor] assigned to every family a parcel of land, according to the proportion of their number, for that end,…and ranged all boys and youth under some family.[24]

In regard to this last statement, it may be helpful for you to understand that, at this point, there were many orphans in the community. Why was this the case? Exactly 50 percent of those who came over on the *Mayflower* died in the first year, either on the journey or living offshore on the ship in very poor conditions. The situation in the Plymouth colony itself was no better, with a lack of shelter and rampant illness. As a result, there were a lot of children without parents who had to be taken in by a surviving family.

> This had very good success, for it made all hands very industrious, so as much more corn was planted than otherwise would have been by any means the Governor or any other could use, and saved him a great deal of trouble, and gave far better content. The women now went willingly into the field, and took their little ones with them to set [plant] corn.[25]

CONFLICT AND SURVIVAL

The problem with the financial backers who forced this communal agreement upon them was an assumption that everybody in the community would simply work willingly for everybody else, with no self-interest. But this idea came into conflict—as it always does—with the sovereignty of individual families. They were dealing with the basic flaw in "collectivism," as Bradford describes it here:

> For this community (so far as it was) [this communal living] was found to breed much confusion and discontent and retard much employment…. For the young men, that were most able and fit for labour and service, did repine [complain] that they should spend their time and strength to work for other men's wives and children without any recompense. The strong… had no more in division of victuals and clothes than he that was weak and not able to do a quarter the other could; this was thought injustice. The aged and graver men…[who were] equalized in labours and victuals, clothes, etc., with the meaner and younger sort, thought it some indignity and disrespect unto them. And for men's wives to be commanded to do service for other men, as dressing their meat, washing their clothes, etc., they deemed it a kind of slavery, neither could many husbands well brook [tolerate] it. [In other words, one husband wouldn't like seeing his wife washing another husband's clothes.] Upon

the point all being to have alike, and all to do alike, they thought themselves in the like condition, and one as good as another; and so, if it did not cut off those relations that God hath set amongst men, yet it did at least much diminish and take off the mutual respects that should be preserved amongst them.[26]

Seeing the inherent problems in this collectivism, they changed the rules of the community. They let every family till its own field and manage its own affairs. Bradford's next comment is rather interesting:

Let none object this is men's corruption, and nothing to the course itself. I answer, seeing all men have this corruption in them, God in His wisdom saw another course fitter for them.[27]

In other words, Bradford was saying that since this is how human nature is, there is a point beyond which you cannot change that behavior. So, the solution was to deal with it realistically. In my experience of counseling with people who have lived in communes in modern times, their testimony indicated exactly the same problems. Isn't it remarkable that many of the major motivations and decisions that confronted the Pilgrims four hundred years ago still confront us today?

THE THANKSGIVING HARVEST

Most Americans are not aware that, historically, there was a distinction between a harvest festival, first held in the fall (probably October) of 1621 (where the Pilgrims, along with the Wampanoag, gave thanks to God for their provisions), and days of thanksgiving that were for answers to prayer, humiliation, and fasting. The source of our Thanksgiving celebration today in America came from the first, which was not technically called a thanksgiving, although the Pilgrims would have given thanks to God. It was a feast and not a fast. However, most importantly, I want to draw your attention to the general attitude of gratitude among the Pilgrims, particularly for the harvest of 1623, which was saved by prayer and fasting.

We do have an actual eyewitness account by William Bradford of the Thanksgiving of 1623, which I provide for you in the quotes below. In some ways, if the Pilgrims had not practiced prayer and fasting, there might never have been any more Thanksgivings! So, in the years to come, when you celebrate Thanksgiving season, please bear these testimonies in mind. In the following excerpts taken from my book *Shaping History Through Prayer and Fasting*, I mainly quote William Bradford:

> It is not possible to quote the many instances of answered prayer that Bradford recorded, but there is one further instance of a public fast that must be mentioned. In the summer of 1623, the corn crop that the Pilgrims had so carefully planted was threatened
>
>> by a great drought which continued from the third week in May, till about the middle of July, without any rain and with great heat for the

most part, insomuch as the corn began to wither away.... It began to languish sore, and some of the drier grounds were parched like withered hay.... Upon which they set apart a solemn day of humiliation, to seek the Lord by humble and fervent prayer.... And He was pleased to give them a gracious and speedy answer, both to their own and the Indians' admiration [i.e. amazement].... For all the morning, and greatest part of the day, it was clear weather and very hot, and not a cloud or any sign of rain to be seen; yet toward evening it began to overcast and shortly after to rain with such sweet and gentle showers as gave them cause of rejoicing and blessing God.

Normally, if rain had fallen at all in such conditions, it would have been in the form of a thunderstorm, which would have beaten down the corn and destroyed the last hope of a harvest. But on this occasion, Bradford went on to relate,

It came without either wind or thunder or any violence, and by degrees [that is, gradually] in that abundance as that the earth was thoroughly...soaked therewith. Which did so apparently revive and quicken the decayed corn and other fruits, as was wonderful to see, and made the Indians astonished to behold [because

> they knew well this was contrary to nature].
> And afterwards the Lord sent them such seasonable showers, with interchange of fair warm weather as, through His blessing, caused a fruitful and liberal harvest.... For which mercy, in time convenient, they also set apart a day of thanksgiving.[28]

It is my belief that this was the first official day of Thanksgiving, which they set apart. So again, please bear in mind—no prayer and fasting, no thanksgiving!

A FOUNDATION OF FASTING

God responded to the Pilgrims' observance of a solemn day of prayer and fasting by sending "sweet and gentle showers" that saved the harvest that year. This event had a lasting impact on the colony, as I point out in the following excerpt from *Shaping History*:

> This practice of setting aside special days of prayer and fasting became an accepted part of the life of Plymouth Colony. On November 15, 1636, a law was passed allowing the governor and his assistants "to command solemn days of humiliation by fasting, etc. and also for thanksgiving as occasion shall be offered."[29]

In other words, the practice of public collective prayer and fasting was built into the Pilgrim community. It became a regular part of their life and was, in fact, part of their laws. In Isaiah 58, there are promises given to those who practice the kind of fasting that is approved by God. These promises come to their climax in verse 12:

> *Those from among you shall build the old waste places; you shall raise up the foundations of many generations; and you shall be called the Repairer of the Breach, the Restorer of Streets to Dwell In.* (Isaiah 58:12)

Here is my closing comment on this subject in *Shaping History*:

> History has demonstrated that the results of fasting promised in this verse were achieved by the Pilgrims. Both spiritually and politically, they "*raise*[d] *up the foundations of many generations.*" Four centuries later, the people of the United States are still building on the foundations that the Pilgrims laid.[30]

It is important for us to recognize that the Pilgrims laid this foundation by prayer and fasting. In the same way, it is time for us to raise up the foundation for future generations. Here is the question we must face: Are we up to the task?

ELEVEN

RETURNING TO THE ROCK

At the beginning of this book, we asked a question: What was the initial "seed" planted by our Pilgrim ancestors that grew into the nation of America, making it a beacon of light and hope for the world?

In many ways, the entire story of the Pilgrims follows the biblical pattern God established from the very beginning of creation in Genesis. I am referring to the key principle we discussed in the earliest pages of our study: that of sowing "seed." This unchanging principle is captured in the following phrase: *"Whatever a man sows, that he will also reap"* (Galatians 6:7).

In this chapter, I will offer a few observations on the principles at work in the lives of this small group of Christians.

FOUNDATIONAL SEEDS

So again, what was the initial seed the Pilgrims sowed? Clearly, from their earliest days in England, the *seed* was *God's Word*. For the Pilgrims, their pure devotion to the Word of God meant risking persecution by separating themselves from the state church and establishing home prayer groups.

1. Being Set Apart

Holiness always requires being "set apart." At the Pilgrims' time in history, separating themselves from the state church so they could be true to their convictions was a radical step for these humble Christians. Clearly, it would end up costing them everything. Yet this became the seed of the foundational principle of the American way of life—and it opened the way for freedom of worship. The freedom of worship in America is unparalleled in any other country in the history of the world. But it came at a price.

What has happened to being "set apart"—to being *holy*? My impression is that, around the time of World War II, the subject of holiness just dropped out of the thinking of Western churches. In fact, even the word *holiness* seemed to disappear from modern-day vocabulary. Now, more than ever, we need to find our way back to an understanding of what it means to be holy.

2. Entering into Covenant

Another principle we see in the lives of the Pilgrims is their amazing understanding of how God views covenant.

They realized that the commitment in a covenant is not merely to God; it is also to one another. When outside forces could have torn them apart, this covenantal commitment held them together.

In our modern times, we need to come back to this idea of covenant. God honors those who keep covenant. An inability to keep covenantal promises is at the very heart of many core issues that are now confronting society. Without the strength of covenantal bonds, we are overwhelmed by forces that are against us.

Here is the key question: Are people—especially Christians—willing to be committed to one another in a specific way? It is interesting to note that, if you study church history, you will find that many of the groups and movements that made a real impact were based on a covenant. The Methodists are an outstanding example.

3. Having Collective Prayer and Fasting

We also saw a deep devotion across the Pilgrim community to collective prayer and fasting, and to the sanctity of the family. As we saw in the account of the Thanksgiving of 1623, the practice of prayer and fasting was absolutely essential to the very survival of the Pilgrims.

The issue that is confronting us today is the survival of the family. Personally, I am convinced that the family *must* win out. I believe it is the sacrosanct unit of society. The family is pivotal to God's purposes, and it must not be violated.

My personal conviction is that the church needs to return to these disciplines of collective prayer and fasting. I promise you this: it will weed out "the men from the boys" and "the women from the girls." If our society is to turn around, we are going to need strong men and women to take up the fight. This will mean implementing the same disciplines we observed in the lives of the Pilgrims: being devoted to God's Word, pursuing holiness, and living in covenantal community, all of which is undergirded by collective prayer and fasting.

WHERE ARE WE NOW?

The nobility of the Pilgrims—the strength, piety, and humility that marked their lives—has been in short supply in recent decades among leaders in nations around the world. How have we sunk so low? How have we fallen from the heights seen in former times?

Much of the Bible's teaching on the purposes of God in history is found in the book of Job. We would do well to look at several passages from Job 12:

> *With Him* [God] *are wisdom and strength, He has counsel and understanding. If He breaks a thing down, it cannot be rebuilt; if He imprisons a man, there can be no release.* [Have you ever gotten in a situation where God shuts you up, and there is no opening?] *If He withholds the waters, they dry up; if He sends them out, they overwhelm the earth. With Him are strength*

and prudence. The deceived and the deceiver are His. He leads counselors away plundered, and makes fools of the judges. (Job 12:13–17)

This portion of Job 12 seems to be an apt comment on recent history. How many nations have been cursed by foolish judgment—the most ridiculous and illogical decisions? That phenomenon is part of God's judgment for disobedience and waywardness. God judges us through our rulers.

It is interesting to read this passage in *The Living Bible*. Although this may not be an entirely accurate translation, many of its phrases are up-to-date, and they help with our understanding.

But true wisdom and power are God's. He alone knows what we should do; He understands. And how great is His might! What He destroys can't be rebuilt. When He closes in on a man, there is no escape. He withholds the rain, and the earth becomes a desert; He sends the storms and floods the ground. Yes, with Him is strength and wisdom. Deceivers and deceived are both His slaves. He makes fools of counselors and judges.

(Job 12:13–17 TLB)

Continuing with verses 18–20 in the *New King James Version*, we read:

He loosens the bonds of kings, and binds their waist with a belt. He leads princes away plundered, and overthrows

> *the mighty. He deprives the trusted ones of speech, and takes away the discernment of the elders.*

You see, if the people of a nation displease God by misbehavior or lack of integrity, there will be no wisdom in any of their rulers. God can remove wisdom from them. Let's continue with the passage:

> *He pours contempt on princes, and disarms the mighty. He uncovers deep things out of darkness, and brings the shadow of death to light. He makes nations great, and destroys them; He enlarges nations, and guides them. He takes away the understanding of the chiefs of the people of the earth, and makes them wander in a pathless wilderness. They grope in the dark without light, and He makes them stagger like a drunken man.* (Job 12:21–25)

Is this descriptive of conditions we regularly see and hear among the nations of the world? To me, it is both applicable and appropriate.

FRUITFUL OR BARREN?

We continue our discussion of a nation's condition as described in Psalm 107. This psalm is one that unfolds God's dealings in history.

> *Oh, that men would give thanks to the LORD for His goodness, and for His wonderful works to the children of men! Let them exalt Him also in the assembly of the*

people, and praise Him in the company of the elders. He turns rivers into a wilderness, and the watersprings into dry ground; a fruitful land into barrenness, for the wickedness of those who dwell in it. (Psalm 107:31–34)

Isn't that remarkable? A nation can be the most beautiful, fruitful, fertile country. But if its people are wicked, God will make it barren. I believe the whole of the North African desert (where I spent three weary years during my service in WWII) is evidence of that condition in history. At one time, that area was fertile forest. But man persistently disobeyed and grieved God and His laws, so God finally changed it. Let's pick up the narrative at verse 35, as the psalm continues:

He turns a wilderness into pools of water, and dry land into watersprings. There He makes the hungry dwell, that they may establish a city for a dwelling place [Bradford quotes this about the Pilgrims], *and sow fields and plant vineyards, that they may yield a fruitful harvest. He also blesses them, and they multiply greatly; and He does not let their cattle decrease. When they are diminished and brought low through oppression, affliction, and sorrow* [i.e., God can enlarge a nation, make it mighty and prosperous; or He can bring it down, humble it, oppress it, and afflict it], *He pours contempt on princes, and causes them to wander in the wilderness where there is no way; yet He sets the poor on high, far from affliction, and makes their families like a flock. The righteous see it and rejoice, and all iniquity stops its mouth. Whoever is*

> *wise will observe these things, and they will understand the lovingkindness of the LORD.* (Psalm 107:35–43)

In that last phrase, the Hebrew word translated "*lovingkindness*" is *chesed*. This word is always related to *a covenant*. My personal translation of the last phrase of this psalm would be "God's covenant-keeping faithfulness." Some would translate this phrase as the "tender affectionate love of God." The important point I want to make about the word *chesed* is that it is always based on *a covenant*. We saw this in a previous chapter with the quotation from Psalm 50:5: "*Gather My saints together to Me, those who have made a covenant with Me by sacrifice.*"

Please notice from this verse that, to be a saint, you have to be in a covenantal relationship with God—based on a sacrifice. What is the sacrifice upon which our covenant is based? Jesus's death on the cross.

In Psalm 50:5, the word "*saints*" is directly related to the word *chesed*. Such a person is one who trusts in God. Do you see the connection? A saint is one who accepts God's covenant-keeping faithfulness. That acceptance is what makes a person a saint—a true, devoted believer in God.

Would you place yourself in that category? Is that a description that applies to you?

TWELVE

STAYING THE COURSE

In the previous chapter, we examined the insights of Psalm 107 as they pertain to the history of a nation. This passage helps us to understand that if we look at the narratives of civilizations down through the centuries—with eyes illuminated by the Holy Spirit and instructed by the Scriptures—we see the covenant-keeping faithfulness of God to the nations. The whole of history unfolds this most important fact: God *never* breaks His covenant. *"My covenant I will not break,"* He says, *"nor alter the word that has gone out of My lips"* (Psalm 89:34).

DIVINE FAVOR

There are many ways to view history. We can view it as a series of mechanical processes, such as Marxism does, or as being cyclical, such as the ancient Greeks did. Or we can view it in the light of the revelation of God in Scripture. If we view history and the destiny of nations in the light of Scripture, this is what shines forth: *the eternal faithfulness of our covenant-keeping God.*

I believe this is why the United States, for many years, has enjoyed divine favor. It is God's covenant-keeping faithfulness. Without question, what the Pilgrims sowed, America has reaped. What the Pilgrims sowed has gone down into the earth, and it has produced an abundant harvest.

The confirmation of this principle appears in Isaiah 61:11, a verse we examined earlier in this book:

For as the earth brings forth its bud, as the garden causes the things that are sown in it to spring forth, so the Lord God will cause righteousness and praise to spring forth before all the nations.

What was sown by the Pilgrims in American history is now springing forth. I believe it will bring righteousness and praise to God before all nations. (For me, as a Britisher, to believe that and proclaim it is something of a miracle. Are you aware that it isn't always easy for the British to appreciate Americans?)

A PICTURE OF PURPOSE

The divine favor America has experienced as a result of the faithful Pilgrims was always intended to touch the nations of the world. Bradford and his companions firmly believed this, as indicated in their writings. As we come to the end of this book, I want to highlight a quote by William Bradford that conveys the true purpose of the Pilgrims.

Unmistakably, the Pilgrims became major instruments in the hands of God in promoting His kingdom throughout this world. We see this so plainly in the following account Bradford gives of the arrival of the *Mayflower* at Cape Cod:

> What could now sustain them but the Spirit of God and His grace? May not…the children of these fathers rightly say: "Our fathers were Englishmen which came over this great ocean, and were ready to perish in this wilderness; but they cried unto the Lord, and He heard their voice and looked on their adversity".… [This is Bradford's own paraphrase of Deuteronomy 26:5–7.] "Let them therefore praise the Lord, because He is good: and His mercies endure forever." "Yea, let them which have been redeemed of the Lord, shew how He hath delivered them from the hand of the oppressor. When they wandered in the desert wilderness out of the way, and found no city to dwell in, both hungry and thirsty, their soul was overwhelmed in them. Let them confess before the Lord His lovingkindness and His wonderful works before the sons of men."[31]

In essence, the second part of this quote is Bradford's own version of Psalm 107:1–5, 8—a summation of the righteous impact the people of God can have upon the destiny of a nation.

A PRAYER OF COMMITMENT

Do you have a desire to see that kind of impact upon the future and destiny of America and other nations of the world? Is that your hope?

If this historical account of the Pilgrims has moved your heart—as it did mine when I first encountered it—I believe it would be good for us to make some kind of a response. As we close this book, would you be willing to join me in a prayer of commitment to follow God's ways as the Pilgrims did?

> God, our Father in heaven, I am moved by the devotion of the Pilgrims to You and Your purposes. Father, I acknowledge Your goodness and faithfulness. I believe You are the eternal, covenant-keeping God.
>
> You have drawn aside the veil over human history and revealed—in Your Word and in this account of the Pilgrims—principles upon which You keep Your covenant. I believe what is said of You in the Bible—that You show mercy to thousands of those who love You and keep Your commandments, and that what You have sown in human history will come forth in a harvest.
>
> Lord, I believe I am living in the harvest hour. I pray for a harvest to come forth in the United States and

in nations all around the world, sown by faithful servants over the centuries, watered by tears, prayers, and sacrifices. In this hour of history, I want to be counted among Your faithful servants, and I present myself to You now.

Thank You, Lord, for the blessings You have granted already to the United States and other nations. I also thank You for the blessings that are yet to come through Your eternal faithfulness. In this hour, I dedicate myself to You—to do whatever You would have me do to fulfill Your purposes in the earth. I pray this in the name of Jesus Christ. Amen.

NOTES

Epigraph

William Bradford, *Of Plymouth Plantation*, ed. Samuel Eliot Morison (New York: Random House, 1952), 47. (Hereafter, citations for *Of Plymouth Plantation* will be designated as *Plymouth*.)

Foreword

1. *Plymouth*, 61.
2. *Plymouth*, 236.

Introduction: A Story That Must Be Told

3. Ronald Reagan, "Farewell Address to the Nation," January 11, 1989, https//www.reaganfoundation.org/media/128652/farewell.pdf.

Chapter Five: How I Met the Pilgrims

4. Derek Prince, *Shaping History Through Prayer and Fasting* (New Kensington, PA: Whitaker House, 1972, 2002, 2018), 155–157. (Hereafter, citations for *Shaping History Through Prayer and Fasting* will be designated as *Shaping History*. All notations in brackets within quotations are by Derek Prince.)

Chapter Six: Key Pilgrim Leaders

5. The first governor was John Carver, who died in April 1621.
6. Samuel Eliot Morison, introduction to *Of Plymouth Plantation* by William Bradford, ed. Samuel Eliot Morison (New York: Random House, 1952), xxiii.
7. *Plymouth*, xxiii.
8. *Plymouth*, xxiii.

Chapter Seven: Pilgrim or Puritan?

9. *Shaping History*, 158–159.
10. Leonard Bacon, *The Genesis of the New England Churches* (New York: Harper and Brothers, 1874), x, as cited in *Shaping History*, 159.
11. *Shaping History*, 159.
12. *Plymouth*, 3, as cited in *Shaping History*, 160.
13. *Plymouth*, 6.

Chapter Eight: The Covenant Concept

14. *Plymouth*, 9.
15. *Plymouth*, 19.
16. *Plymouth*, 25.

Chapter Nine: How the Pilgrims Prevailed

17. *Plymouth*, 47.
18. *Shaping History*, 161–162.
19. Edward Winslow, quoted in Verna M. Hall, *Christian History of the Constitution* (San Francisco, CA: The American Constitution Press, 1960), 184, as cited in *Shaping History*, 162–163. Additional bracketed comments were inserted by Derek Prince into the quotations for this book.
20. Winslow, quoted in *Christian History*, 184, as cited in *Shaping History*, 163.
21. Winslow, quoted in *Christian History*, 184, as cited in *Shaping History*, 163.
22. *Shaping History*, 163.

Chapter Ten: The Pilgrims in Community

23. *Plymouth*, 120.
24. *Plymouth*, 120.
25. *Plymouth*, 120.
26. *Plymouth*, 121.
27. Plymouth, 121.
28. *Shaping History*, 164–165. (Quotations from *Plymouth*, 131–132.)
29. *Shaping History*, 165. (Quotation from *Plymouth*, 132, footnote 1.)
30. *Shaping History*, 166.

Chapter Twelve: Staying the Course

31. *Plymouth*, 62–63, as cited in *Shaping History*, 164.

ABOUT THE AUTHOR

Derek Prince (1915–2003) was born in India of British parents. He was educated as a scholar of Greek and Latin at Eton College and King's College, Cambridge, in England. Upon graduation, he held a fellowship (equivalent to a professorship) in Ancient and Modern Philosophy at King's College. Prince also studied Hebrew, Aramaic, and modern languages at Cambridge and the Hebrew University in Jerusalem. As a student, he was a philosopher and a self-proclaimed agnostic.

While serving in the Royal Army Medical Corps (RAMC) during World War II, Prince began to study the Bible as a philosophical work. Converted through a powerful encounter with Jesus Christ, he was baptized in the Holy Spirit a few days later. Out of this encounter, he formed two conclusions: first, that Jesus Christ is alive; second, that the Bible is a true, relevant, up-to-date book. These conclusions altered the whole course of his life, which he then devoted to studying and teaching the Bible as the Word of God.

Discharged from the army in Jerusalem in 1945, he married Lydia Christensen, founder of a children's home there. Upon their marriage, he immediately became father to Lydia's eight adopted daughters—six Jewish, one Palestinian Arab, and one English. Together, the family saw the rebirth of the state of Israel in 1948. In the late 1950s, they adopted another daughter while Prince was serving as principal of a teachers' training college in Kenya.

In 1963, the Princes immigrated to the United States and pastored a church in Seattle. In 1973, Prince became one of the founders of Intercessors for America. His book *Shaping History Through Prayer and Fasting* has awakened Christians around the world to their responsibility to pray for their governments. Many consider underground translations of the book as instrumental in the fall of communist regimes in the USSR, East Germany, and Czechoslovakia.

Lydia Prince died in 1975, and Prince married Ruth Baker (a single mother to three adopted children) in 1978. He met his second wife, like his first wife, while she was serving the Lord in Jerusalem. Ruth died in December 1998 in Jerusalem, where they had lived since 1981.

Until a few years before his own death in 2003 at the age of eighty-eight, Prince persisted in the ministry God had called him to as he traveled the world, imparting God's revealed truth, praying for the sick and afflicted, and sharing his prophetic insights into world events in the light of Scripture. Internationally recognized as a Bible scholar and spiritual patriarch, Derek Prince established a teaching ministry that spanned six continents and more than sixty years. He is the author of more than eighty books, six hundred audio teachings, and one hundred video teachings, many of which have been translated and published in more than one hundred languages. He pioneered teaching on such groundbreaking themes as generational curses, the biblical significance of Israel, and demonology.

Prince's radio program, which began in 1979, has been translated into more than a dozen languages and continues to touch lives. Derek Prince's main gift of explaining the Bible and its teachings in a clear and simple way has helped build a foundation of faith in millions of lives. His nondenominational, nonsectarian approach has made his teaching equally relevant and helpful to people from all racial and religious backgrounds, and his messages are estimated to have reached more than half the globe.

In 2002, he said, "It is my desire—and I believe the Lord's desire—that this ministry continue the work, which God began through me over sixty years ago, until Jesus returns."

Derek Prince Ministries continues to reach out to believers in over 140 countries with Derek's teaching, fulfilling the mandate to keep on "until Jesus returns." This is accomplished through the outreaches of more than forty-five Derek Prince offices around the world, including primary work in Australia,

Canada, China, France, Germany, the Netherlands, New Zealand, Norway, Russia, South Africa, Switzerland, the United Kingdom, and the United States. For current information about these and other worldwide locations, visit www.derekprince.org.